The Tao of Love

The Tao of Love

Ed Bremson

iUniverse, Inc.
New York Lincoln Shanghai

The Tao of Love

iUniverse, Inc.

For information address:
iUniverse, Inc.
2021 Pine Lake Road, Suite 100
Lincoln, NE 68512
www.iuniverse.com

ISBN: 0-595-30475-3

Printed in the United States of America

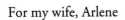

For my wife, Arlene

The Tao of Love

Prologue

Many things have been written and said about love over the years. There are even several books with the title *The Tao of Love*. I didn't consult any of those for this book. Rather, I relied on the 1891 James Legge translation of the *Tao Te Ching*, written by Lao Tzu, a Chinese philosopher who lived before the time of Christ. The *Tao Te Ching* is a book of religious wisdom and advice. Its verses reflect particular views on life. Those views can be interpreted as they apply to many things. In this case I interpreted them as they apply to love. The ideas contained herein are partly mine and partly those of Lao Tzu. I don't claim that I have said all there is to say about this subject, but I do hope I have provoked some discussion. I thank James Legge for providing me with such an interesting, stimulating, and accessible translation.

If you can point to it
And call it "Love,"
It is not love.
Love exists
As an idea exists.
You can't point to an idea.
You can only point
To its manifestation.
So it is with love.

Love exists
With or without desire.
One day you look
At your lover,
Feeling no desire,
And you find
Yourself saying
"I love you."
Desire may follow,
But desire is desire,
Not love.

Love is wonderful because
We don't need to know hate
In order to know love.
In fact, hate and love
Are so antithetical
To each other that,
If you feel one,
You can't feel the other.

Sometimes it seems
That you have no existence
Apart from the object
Of your love.
This is not love.
It is obsession,
Or infatuation.
In love, you are
Fully existent,
Fully aware of yourself
As separate,
And yet fully absorbed
In your lover
And your love.
It truly is
The best of all worlds.

Just as musical tones
Depend on each other
To create beautiful harmonies,
The best love
Is fully requited,
And it sings.

The lover
Doesn't have to do anything
To be loved.
Flowers are nice.
Gifts are nice.
But giving of yourself
Is more important by far.
And being open to love
Allows love to grow.

Open yourself up,
Like an empty vessel,
So that when love
Comes flowing in,
Like a river,
You can let yourself
Be filled.

How can a person
Love a porcupine?
If you would know love,
Put away your quills.

Thinking about love
Can lead to paradox
And apparent
Contradiction,
Which must be accepted,
Just as your lover
Must be accepted,
At some point,
Without further analysis.

Love makes
Two people shine
Much brighter
Than they ever shone
Alone.

Lovers do not act
From a wish
To be benevolent,
But rather from an impulse
To express the love
They are feeling
Inside.

Two lovers may be
In different cities,
And yet the power
Of their love
Remains as great
As when they occupy
The same bed.

Love loses nothing
When it is expressed.
If anything,
It gains substance
And power
To be expressed
Again.

Men and women
Are mysteries
To each other
Until love happens,
Then no more.

Love is long-enduring
Because lovers
Do not live
For themselves alone.
By putting yourself last,
You find yourself first,
At least in the mind
Of your lover.

Just as water
Flows downhill
To the lowest place,
The best position in love
Is the lowest position,
Not just for the body,
Or for the mind,
But for every part
Of your being.
Submitting yourself
To your lover
Is the greatest good.

To withdraw into obscurity
With your lover
Is the way of love.
In a crowded room,
On a deserted beach,
With eyes for
Each other
Alone,
The world goes by
Around you,
And for awhile
You could not care less.
Would that you
Could live that way
Forever.

Love makes
All things possible,
And yet is not possessive.
Love does all things,
And yet is not boastful.
Love guides all actions,
And yet does not control them.
This is the mysterious quality
Of love.

It is easier
For a full heart
To grow
Than an empty one.

The more you think about love,
The less you understand it.
Love should be experienced.
Then there are
No more questions,
Only answers.

Some people fear
Feeling love
Because they fear
The pain and anguish
Of losing love.
Who can blame them?
There may be
No greater pain
Than the pain of loss.
But those who are
Still feeling fear
Are probably
Still feeling pain.
They should wait.

Love cannot be
Seen or heard,
Or held in your hand.
It cannot be described,
But it can be known.
And oh what joy
It can bring.

Love can be known,
But we can
Also be mistaken,
Thinking love is there
When it's not.
What unhappiness
That can bring.

Love is not like Rocket Science.
You can only understand it
With your heart,
Not your mind.

If you would
Flourish in love,
Don't be too full
Of yourself,
And much
About yourself
Will be forgiven.

Everything has
A beginning,
A middle,
And an end,
Even love.
And every end
Is also a beginning.

Whoever possesses love
Possesses part of Heaven,
And retains
A youthful quality
That those who
Do not possess love
Can never know.

Those who do not
Know love
May also
Not know faith,
And are the poorer
Because of it.

People in love
Are nicer to other people.
They tend to do what's right.
They eschew hypocrisy,
Are loyal, and strive always
To create harmony.
We need more lovers.

Pride gets in the way
Of many things,
Including love.
Avoid pride
As you would
A contagion.
They are both unhealthy.

If everyone
Chose to be
Always kind,
Instead of
Sometimes mean,
There'd be more room
For love.

I may seem stupid
And in a state of chaos.
I may seem
Dull and confused.
Others may seem
To be brilliant,
While my mind
May seem far away.
Excuse me, please,
I'm in love.

So much good
Comes from love.
But who can tell
The nature of love?
It eludes our sight.
It eludes our touch.
We know it's there,
But we don't know where.
All we know:
Love never decays.

In love,
The partial becomes complete;
The empty becomes full;
The worn out becomes new.
And in many ways
Love sets you free.

The lover holds
In his grasp
Something that
Few people have,
But everyone wants.
And everything about
His being proclaims,
"This is what's possible
With love."

You can't make love
Last forever,
But you can make it
Wither and die.

We are helpless
In the face of love.
But whatever
We surrender
Is more than amply
Repaid.

There are lots of things
That love is not.
But can anyone say
What love is?
That's easier asked
Than answered.

Something undefined
And complete
Came into existence
Under Heaven.
How still and formless
It was,
Reaching everywhere,
Changeless, inexhaustible.
And I called it Love.

Love leaves no trace
Of wheels or footsteps,
As it passes,
For everyone to see.
But wherever it goes,
Lovers feel the poetry of it
Written on their hearts.

Just as yin contains
A little bit of yang,
And yang
A little bit of yin,
So man contains
A little bit of woman,
And woman
A little bit of man,
All the better to
Love and understand
Each other.

He who tries to find love
By actively seeking it
Most likely will not succeed.
Love is spiritual.
He who would gain it,
Destroys it.
He who would hold it,
Loses it.
Stop trying so hard.
Let love happen.

Love matures,
But it does not grow old.
Love ends,
But it does not grow stale.
We grow stale.
We may turn our backs on love,
But love never turns
Its back on us.

With love,
We wouldn't need
So many laws.
Lovers don't kill,
Not really.
And they don't lie or steal.
We're all better people
With love.

With love,
We can do anything,
Or at least
We think we can,
Which amounts
To the same thing.
Let us fill the world
With love,
And then see
Where our deeds
May take us.

When you
Lose yourself
In love,
You gain
Much more
Than was lost.

Love is everywhere.
It has accomplished
Some wonderful things.
Left alone,
It would accomplish
Even more.
But that's the problem:
It's not always
Left alone.

We all want
To be close to lovers,
As if their happiness
Might rub off on us.
Would that it was
So easy,
But love doesn't
Work that way.

If love could be got
For the taking,
The world would be
A different place.
We all know
That's not going to happen,
But it's nice to think
It might.

It has been said,
"There are more fish
In the sea."
But what good
Does that do
After you lose
The fish
That belonged to you?

You must abide by
The insubstantial
And eschew
That which is solid;
Dwell with the flower
And not with the fruit,
If you would know love.

Love is like
The air we breathe.
It is the same for everyone:
The man on the street,
The girl in the shop,
And even for
Princes and queens.

They say that
Opposites attract.
I think an opposite
Completes.
And the same is true
Of love.

Love makes you laugh,
And what better tonics
For the soul
Than laughter
And love?

Love can't be known
By the senses.
You have to be in love
In order to see love.

Some things are increased
By being diminished,
While some things are diminished
By being increased.
And love often works
That way.

Love does nothing,
Yet accomplishes great things.
It softens the hardest heart.
It teaches without words.
When the weak
Overcome the strong,
Love is there.

He who devotes himself
To the world
Seeks to gain
All that the world
Has to offer.
He who devotes himself
To love
Seeks to give
All that he has
To give.

Whoever is content
Will live long.
Love can make you
Content.

Discontentment
Leads to calamity.
Avoid calamity.
Hold fast
To love.

Lovers have
No minds of their own.
They belong to each other,
With no thoughts
Of anything but
Each other.

All good things
Come from love,
And are nourished
In its out flowing
Glow.

When love is nourished,
When love grows,
The whole world,
Far and wide,
Knows it,
Feels it,
And is better
Because of it.
And all this begins
In the hearts of
Two people.

Whoever knows love
Is like a child
Who sees the world
Through eyes
Full of wonder,
And who finds joy
In the smallest
Of things.

It is not necessary
To speak of love,
Because you
Show your love,
Every day,
In many ways.

In everyday existence,
Happiness and misery
May be found
Side by side.
But this is not so
With love.

You can't have
Moderation in love
And still have love.
Love is like
A total surrender.

Love is like
A food
That gives
Essential nutrients
To the soul
Instead of
To the body.

Love prospers better
When two people
Approach each other
As equals.

Love wipes away
All the past,
And focuses
Only on today.

Lovers do things
That may not
Seem so great
In the eyes of the world.
But in the eyes of love,
And in the beating of two hearts,
They are the grandest things
Of all.

Love, like a tree,
Grows from a tiny seed
And becomes
What it becomes;
And no one can say
It should be otherwise.

In love,
You don't have to think.
In fact,
The less you use
Your mind,
The better.
No need for
Planning or guessing,
Only feeling and being.
Love comes from
The heart.

In love, there are
Many precious things
To prize and hold onto;
But the greatest of these
Is love itself.

Whoever tries to gain
The upper hand in love
Will be lucky
To know love
At all.

It is difficult
For one individual
To know another;
But it's easy
With love.

Love helps us
Know many things
That we could never
Otherwise know.

You don't have to be
On your guard
With love.
True, something bad
May happen,
But something wonderful
May happen
Too.

Everyone knows
You get farther
With kindness
Than with anything else;
But no one is able
To carry it out
In practice,
Except for those
In love.

It is impossible to say
Which is the oldest emotion,
But love has remained constant
Throughout all time.
It is the same today
As it was a million
Days ago.
It will be the same tomorrow,
And for a million tomorrows.
And it is there
For us alone
To know.

Love is easily experienced
Once we get beyond
All that is not love.

Love is mysterious
And not easily understood,
But we really wouldn't want it
Any other way.

Don't wait until
You lose love
To find out
What love is.

After speaking about love
For a long, long time,
With fine words and phrases,
Some even in rhyme,
I realize how little
I know.

Epilogue

Love is an important and necessary force in the world today. Anything we can do to shed light on it and help it prosper is good. That was my intention in writing this book. I wanted to add my voice and the voice of Lao Tzu to the discussion in hopes that it might help in some way. Only the reader can decide whether or not I have succeeded.

0-595-30475-3

Made in the USA
Middletown, DE
15 October 2021